LEAD
YOUR FAMILY
LIKE JESUS

**POWERFUL PARENTING PRINCIPLES
FROM THE CREATOR OF FAMILIES**

FOCUS ON THE FAMILY

Tyndale House Publishers, Inc.
Carol Stream, Illinois

CONTENTS

QUICK START GUIDE FOR PARENTS

Whether you're studying in a group, as a couple, or individually, this book is for you. It's packed with discussion questions, advice, biblical input, and application activities.

But maybe all you'd like to do right now is watch the accompanying video and talk about it with your spouse —or think about it on your own. If so, go directly to the "Watch This!" section of each chapter. There you'll find the discussion questions you're looking for.

When you have more time, we encourage you to explore the other features in this book. We think you'll find them family-changing!

WELCOME!

If there's anything you don't need, it's one more thing to do.

Unless, of course, that one thing might make the *other* things a whole lot easier.

We can't guarantee that this video series will take all the challenge out of parenthood. It won't keep your kids from forgetting their lunch money, make them trade in their video games for art museum passes, or remind them to scoop the cat's litter box.

But it *will* help you understand why leading your family is so crucial, how to follow the servant leadership example of Jesus, and how to enjoy the journey to the fullest. In other words, you'll discover how to be the mom or dad you really want to be.

That takes effort, but it doesn't take boredom or busy work. So we've designed this course to be provocative and practical. At its heart is a powerful, down-to-earth video series featuring three parents with plenty of experience in walking the leadership trail Jesus blazed. And in your hands is the book that's going to make it all personal for you—the Participant's Guide.

In each chapter of this book, you'll find the following sections:

Grand Opening. Read this brief excerpt to focus on the subject at hand.

Watch This! Use this section as you view and think about the video; it includes thought-provoking questions and biblical input.

So What? Practice makes perfect, so here's your chance to begin applying principles from the video to your own family.

Your Turn. To wrap up, you'll find encouragement and a challenge for the week.

Whether you're using this book as part of a group or on your own, taking a few minutes to read and complete each chapter will bring the messages of the video home.

And isn't that exactly where you need it most?

Note: Many issues addressed in this series are difficult ones. Some parents may need to address them in greater detail and depth. The video presentations and this guide are intended as general advice only, and not to replace clinical counseling, medical treatment, legal counsel, or pastoral guidance.

Focus on the Family maintains a referral network of Christian counselors. For information, call 1-800-A-FAMILY and ask for the counseling department. You can also find plenty of parenting advice and encouragement at www.focusonthefamily.com.

CHAPTER 1
To Lead Is to Serve

THE POINT: Jesus wants us to be servant leaders in our families, and showed us how.

GRAND OPENING
Getting Your Thoughts Together

Under the Influence
by Ken Blanchard

By looking at Jesus, you can learn how to build a loving relationship with your spouse, children, and extended family—no matter how you were raised and no matter what challenges your family faces.

Those challenges are all around us. In too many families love has been distorted to "you don't love me unless you [fill in the blank]," rather than the unconditional serving that Jesus modeled. Self-promotion (pride) and self-protection (fear) have replaced love and vulnerability. We're afraid to give our whole hearts to others because we don't want to be hurt. Indifference moves in and intimacy is replaced with isolation.

The good news is that there's a better way. There's a perfect leadership role model you can trust. His name is Jesus. All families matter to Him. The big question is, does Jesus matter in your family? . . .

[Family leaders make] personal choices about how and to what end they will use their influence. When it comes to decisions like these, each of us must decide: *Am I seeking to serve God and the well-being of my family members, or am I seeking my own self-interest?*

When parents lead like Jesus, they serve God and others with love as the ultimate goal. As a result, spouses enjoy greater intimacy and fulfillment, children gain character-building skills and self-worth, and family relationships thrive![1]

Why is it hard to stop "looking out for Number One," even when you're a parent? What do people fear might happen if they do that?

Is it tough to believe that putting the well-being of your family above your own interests could actually benefit you? Why or why not?

WATCH THIS!
Viewing and Discussing the Video

In this portion of the video, Ken Blanchard explains what leadership is: a process of influencing the thinking, behavior, or development of someone else. He reveals that anyone can be a leader, that every parent is a leader, and that leading a family as Jesus would has great benefits.

Tricia Goyer discusses what it means to be a family leader. It doesn't mean controlling everything, being an "expert," or being perfect. It's all about serving—like Jesus. Finally, Phil Hodges describes how Jesus demonstrated loving leadership—and why leading your family as He led isn't an unreachable goal.

After viewing the authors' presentations, use questions like the following to help you think through what you saw and heard.

1. "Any time you seek to influence the thinking, behavior, or development of another person, you take on the role of a leader." That's how Ken Blanchard defines leadership. Is that different from the way you've been defining it? If so, how? And since it puts you as a parent in the "leader" category, which of the following describes your feelings about that?
   - nervous
   - like I just got a promotion
   - like I haven't been doing my job
   - like it's time to fire my kids
   - other _____

2. Read Philippians 2:5-11. Why do you suppose Jesus "did not consider equality with God something to be grasped"? How does that explain why He was a servant leader? When we refuse to

"make ourselves nothing" for the sake of our families, what are we grasping for?

3. Tricia Goyer was an unwed teenage mom. When you know that, how does it affect the way you see her advice on leading your family like Jesus?
   - It doesn't.
   - It reminds me that God gives us second chances, and I'm glad He does.
   - It makes her ideas even more believable, because she's "been there."
   - It makes me less likely to take her advice seriously.
   - other _____

4. Read Luke 1:26–38. On a scale of 1 to 10 (10 being impossible), how hard would it be for you to have Mary's "servant attitude" in each of the following situations? How might having such an attitude influence the way you handle each scenario?
   - Your 19-year-old daughter is arrested for shoplifting a smartphone case, and pleads for you to bail her out of jail.
   - You find yourself in the hospital emergency room with your five-year-old son, who ignored your warnings not to put dried peas in his nose.

- You discover your eight-year-old son viewing pornography on the Internet.
- Your 15-year-old daughter announces that she must have a set of watercolor pencils, six pounds of modeling clay, and a copy of *Hamlet*—at 10 p.m. the night before her English class project is due.

5. How might Phil Hodges' portion of the video be different if this course were based on each of the following books?
   - *Lead Your Family Like Lance Armstrong*
   - *Lead Your Family Like the Taliban*
   - *Lead Your Family Like Tiger Woods*

When it comes to finding a parenting example, where do you think most people look? If you had to convince them to consider Jesus, how would you do it?

6. When Jesus washed His disciples' feet (John 13:1-17), what was He trying to teach them? If He wanted to teach that lesson today to each of the following people, what might He do?

- the weary parent of a newborn
- your oldest child
- your spouse

If you wanted to be a servant to each of the aforementioned people, how would you do it?

 Why I Love the Way Jesus Led
by Phil Hodges

When it comes to humility, Jesus was truly the Master. You've probably heard about the time when, despite His heavenly credentials, He washed His followers' dirty feet. . . .

That was hardly the only time Jesus displayed His humble spirit, however. Early in His ministry, He demonstrated His desire to please only the Father and to turn control of His life over to Him. Jesus made that choice public when He surrendered all to His Father and insisted that John baptize Him "to fulfill all righteousness" (Matthew 3:15).

Sometimes Jesus' desire to please the Father wasn't just a matter of doing something that others might have considered beneath their

---

dignity. He demonstrated this dramatically when He went into the wilderness and was tempted by Satan:

> For the third test, the Devil took him on the peak of a huge mountain. He gestured expansively, pointing out all the earth's kingdoms, how glorious they all were. Then he said, "They're yours—lock, stock, and barrel. Just go down on your knees and worship me, and they're yours."
>
> Jesus' refusal was curt: "Beat it, Satan!" He backed his rebuke with a third quotation from Deuteronomy: "Worship the Lord your God, and only him. Serve him with absolute single-heartedness." (Matthew 4:8 10, MSG)

Jesus repeatedly affirmed *whose He was* and *who He was.* He determined that He would live by the mission His Father had given Him for the accomplishment of His Father's purpose. Jesus could have been prideful; He was the Son of God. He could have been fearful; all the powers of darkness were against Him. Instead, in all these situations, Jesus chose the will of His Father. He chose to lead by serving.[2]

Based on this excerpt, would you say that being humble and being spineless are the same thing? Why or why not? How is it important for family leaders to know the difference?

Foot-Washing: The Next Generation

Cleanup on Aisle 1: Diaper Duty

Your toddler's third birthday is next week. But she can't seem to get potty-trained. A "scientific" potty chair, chocolate-chip bribes, hopeful pep talks—nothing seems to work. You're starting to think she's doing this on purpose; every new diaper is like a nail in your coffin. Based on the example of Jesus in John 13:1-17, how might a servant leader handle this? What might you do to avoid getting resentful and to promote the child's long-term good?

Cleanup on Aisle 2: The Riotous Room

Are you smarter than a fifth-grader? Yes, and tidier, too. Your ten-year-old son's room seems knee-deep in LEGOs, sour gummy worms, and dirty socks. The bed hasn't been made since Pluto was officially a planet, and the smell is starting to make the neighbor's pit bull whimper.

Your blood pressure goes up every time you try in vain to get your son to undo the carnage. You suspect he'd make progress if you offered to man a shovel at his side, but you're hardly in the mood. Based on the example of Jesus in John 13:1-17, how might a servant leader handle this? What might you do to avoid getting resentful and to promote the child's long-term good?

Cleanup on Aisle 3: A Financial Mess

Thanks to your 16 year-old's brief inattention while driving, your Toyota Corolla has acquired a watermelon-sized dent in the hood. The deductible on your insurance guarantees that you're going to pay at least $1,200. Your child's remorse appears genuine, but so is your anger. The annual income of your teen is approximately nothing, other than the $25 Amazon gift card Aunt Samantha sends every Christmas. Cleaning up this mess seems to fall to you. Based on the example of Jesus in John 13:1-17, how might a servant leader handle this? What might you do to avoid getting resentful and to promote the child's long-term good?

How Does It Look to Lead Your Family?
by Tricia Goyer

Leading like Jesus means leading your family with humility. . . . Humility is an attitude that reflects a keen understanding of our limitations. *People with humility don't think less of themselves; they just think of themselves less.* That grows out of having confidence in God. . . .

But how does [this] look in the everyday rush of parenting? I found out during a very busy time of my life.

My calendar was in chaos. I was having trouble making wise choices about my commitments and my family's activities. One night I broke down crying from being overwhelmed.

My husband, John, asked if we could sit down and go over my schedule. He wanted us to look at everything I'd committed to and figure out where the problem was. He started by asking me to make a list of everything I did in a week.

I scoffed. "You don't have enough paper," I said. Feeling a burden heavy on my shoulders, I started going through the list—caring for our home and children, my work projects, my volunteering, my church service, and all the kids' activities.

After everything was listed, John helped me to rate everything on a scale of one through four. The "ones" were things I *had* to do, such as feeding the kids and homeschooling. The "twos" were things I *should* do, like laundry and housecleaning. The "threes" were things I enjoyed doing and that helped me, such as Bible study or exercise class. The fours, I discovered, were things I did because I was afraid to say no, or because I wanted to look good or have my kids look good.

To refocus and get a better handle on my schedule, I cut out all the fours. I even cut out some threes, realizing that even though they were good things, it wasn't the right season for them.

Evaluating my activities helped my schedule, and it gave me a glimpse into my heart. I was trying to get others—even God—to love me because of things I did. I realized, though, that God loves me already. When I focus on Him and His plans for me, I can find peace—and have confidence in the things I choose, knowing I'm doing them for God alone.[3]

This week you can take a step forward in your journey to servant leadership. Try starting with the calendar-clearing exercise Tricia and John Goyer used.

Ask yourself, *Is our schedule designed to serve me or the rest of our family?* List the tasks you perform in a typical week, categorizing them as "ones" (things you have to do), "twos" (things you should do), "threes" (things you enjoy and that benefit you), or "fours" (things you're afraid to say no to). Cut out the fours and at least some of the threes. See how you and your family can grow closer by using some of the time you're saving.

CHAPTER 2
The Heart

THE POINT: Leading your family like Jesus is a spiritual matter; be motivated not by self-interest, but by the betterment of those you're leading.

GRAND OPENING
Getting Your Thoughts Together

Important Forever
by Ken Blanchard

John Ortberg [wrote a] wonderful book, *When the Game Is Over, It All Goes Back in the Box.* John has a marvelous exercise in the book that goes like this:

It's 4:00 in the afternoon and you're getting ready to go home. There are two piles of Post-It® notes on your desk. One says *Important Forever* and the other says *Temporary Stuff.* Put a Post-It from one of the two piles on everything you notice as you leave—the computer, your desk, your administrative assistant, the Coke machine, your receptionist, your car. Then do the same when you get home—on your bicycle, your golf clubs, people, and things in the house. . . .

Jesus knew all about that kind of eternal perspective. . . .

Just knowing about the long-term view wasn't enough for Jesus, of course. Everything He did was about the forever benefits, and He calls us to do the same. . . .

It's easy to focus our time and efforts on things—jobs, houses, activities. But in times like the fire [that burned down our home] we learn that what we carry in our hearts and relationships is what lasts. Margie and I were challenged to hold things loosely and cherish people—particularly our family and one another. We were reminded that God's love is another thing that lasts; a fire can't take it away. . . .

When we lost our house, in the world's eyes we'd lost everything—but Margie and I knew better. We'd spent twenty-five years caring for the things in our home. In the end, Margie and I—and the family we built—are what stood. That's what the foundation of leading your family like Jesus is all about: focusing on who you love and who loves you.

Leading your family like Jesus focuses on what's really important. And it all starts in the heart.[4]

Maybe your house hasn't burned down. But have you ever had an experience that reminded you to treasure family members more and other parts of your life less? If so, how long did that changed perspective last? If it's faded, how do you feel about that?

WATCH THIS!

Viewing and Discussing the Video

In this portion of the video, Ken explains why it's so important for parents to have an eternal perspective. Phil points out why parents should "say no to EGO," or Edging God Out. Instead of letting pride and fear shape their parenting, they need to be humble and trust their heavenly Father as Jesus did. Tricia notes that Jesus-like family leaders don't compare themselves to others; they focus on God instead. Like Jesus, they display a different kind of EGO: Exalting God Only.

After viewing the authors' presentations, use questions like the following to help you think through what you saw and heard.

1. Read Matthew 6:31-34. Which parts of Jesus' teaching here would you say reflect the eternal perspective Ken talks about? Other than the food and clothing mentioned, what are three things parents tend to worry about? How could you rephrase the passage to include those concerns?

2. How might having an "earthly-only" perspective lead the following parents to deal with their situations? How could an eternal perspective change their responses?

- a mom and dad learning that their newborn has Down syndrome
- a dad whose toddler has accidentally flushed a pet hamster down the toilet
- a single mom who can't get her ex-husband to pay child support
- a dad whose teenage daughter has just come home from the mall with purple hair

3. As Phil Hodges explains in the book *Lead Your Family Like Jesus,* he once made a bad investment but wouldn't admit it to his family. When he insisted on investing even more, it hurt his relationship with his wife and kids. How might his experience prove the truth of Proverbs 16:18 and Proverbs 29:25? When it comes to parenting, how might you "put your money" on the wrong "investment," only to regret it later—and refuse to acknowledge it?

4. If God is all-powerful and present everywhere, how is it possible for a parent to "Edge God Out"? Since He doesn't usually strike

people with lightning to alert them to this problem, what early warning signs of EGOmania could parents look for?

5. From best to worst, where would you rank yourself in each of the following trios regarding parenting? Is there any value in doing that? What might Tricia Goyer think of such an exercise?
   - You, "Supernanny" Jo Frost, and King Saul (1 Samuel 20:30-34)
   - You, Bill Cosby, and the father of Adolf Hitler
   - You, Abraham Lincoln's mother, and Marge of *The Simpsons*
   - You, Joseph (Luke 2:39-40), and the mother of Honey Boo Boo

6. When was the last time you "exalted" God? How can a parent "Exalt God Only" in a way that others can't?

Say No to EGO
by Phil Hodges

When we turn from Jesus' humble example and Edge God Out, the trickle-down effect on our children is profound. When pride and fear take possession of our hearts, the damage to our kids is long-lasting and far-reaching. In fact, walking away from God has been the root of dysfunction in families since the beginning of time.

Adam and Eve wanted to be like God. When they succumbed to the temptations of pride and fear, they ended up hiding in the bushes. Their firstborn child, Cain, also took matters into his own hands and killed his younger brother, Abel, in a fit of prideful anger.

As I found when my family investment plan collapsed, family leaders Edge God Out when they trust in something other than God's character and unconditional love as their source of security and self-worth. Prideful or fear-filled parents tend to be quick to judge, quick to take offense, quick to speak, and quick to push blame away and pull praise closer. They embrace what looks good in their eyes—even when, deep down, they know it's not right. . . .

Edging God Out not only affects current family relationships and the character of the next generation, it will also influence generations to come. The Bible tells us that the sins of the fathers will be carried to the third and fourth generation. That's why it's important for parents to imitate the humility of Jesus—and break the chain.[5]

When it comes to parenting, do you ever "trust in something other than God's character and unconditional love as [your] source of security and self-worth"? What might that "something" be? Do you think trusting in God alone would be a relief? Why or why not?

SO WHAT?
Connecting Principles to Parenting

Indicate your answer by marking a spot on the line between one name and the other.

Altaring Your EGO: A Self-Test About Self

1. When it comes to worshiping only God, I'm more like . . .

   _____

   Richard Dawkins, atheist   Billy Graham, evangelist

2. My opinion of myself, my self-esteem, is more like that of . . .

   _____

   Napoleon Bonaparte, megalomaniac   Charlie Brown, perennial
                                                             loser

3. When it comes to bragging, taking the credit, showing off, and demanding all the attention, I'm more like . . .

   _____

   Bart Simpson, brat   Mother Teresa, servant of the poor

4. When it comes to protecting myself by withholding information, intimidating others, hoarding control or money, or discouraging honest feedback, I'm more like . . .

   _____

   Ebenezer Scrooge, miser   Bob Cratchit, bookkeeper

---

5. I compare myself unfavorably with others about as often as . . .

_____

Julius Caesar, would-be god   Ugly Duckling,
"disrespected" fowl

6. Regarding humility, people who know me would say I'm more like . . .

_____

Pharaoh, pyramid builder   Mahatma Gandhi, nonviolent activist

7. My confidence in God's nature, goodness, purpose, plan, process, and provision is like that of . . .

_____

Eeyore, pessimistic donkey   The Apostle Paul, letter writer

8. I seek to lead my family with a higher purpose—beyond "success" and "significance" to obedience and service—much like . . .

_____

Don Vito Corleone, godfather   Abraham, biblical patriarch

9. When it comes to surrendering to what I believe about God, His kingdom, and His claim on my life and leadership, I'm more like . . .

_____

Ananias and Sapphira (Acts 5)   Jim Elliot, martyred missionary

10. I seek the guidance of the Holy Spirit, the ultimate coach, as often as . . .

_____

Judas, famous betrayer   Peter, famous betrayer

Which three of the preceding questions seem to shed the most light on whether you might have an "EGO" problem? How might the final question and answer encourage a parent who fears his imperfections disqualify him from being a servant leader?

An Audience of One
by Tricia Goyer

Even though He *was* God, Jesus didn't lift up His own ego or pride. Instead, He depended on God the Father as His source for everything—including His self-esteem and security. . . .

I often think like this during my morning quiet time, after I've read God's Word and prayed. When His awesomeness is fresh on my mind, I know I'd be foolish to do anything else.

But then, through the day, things change. I don't know about you, but sometimes God is the last person I think about when I get in over my head or when I'm making a decision, big or small. I'm prone to think about myself and looking good to others. I consider:

- What will my neighbor think?
- Will the other moms think I'm a bad mom if I don't [fill in the blank]?

- Will I be the only person at church not volunteering?
- Will my kids feel bad if they don't have what everyone else does?

As you can tell from these questions, when I'm worried about what others think it's because I'm concerned about how I look. I'm afraid I won't measure up. I'm worried about myself more than about what God wants me to do—or who He wants me to be.[6]

Remember John Ortberg's exercise with the sticky notes? This week, instead of labeling the people in your life as "Important Forever" or "Temporary Stuff," put some mental labels on their opinions. Is what your neighbors think of you important forever? How about your old college professor or drill sergeant? Your parents? Your child? God?

If their ratings are really temporary stuff, why work so hard to impress them? On the other hand, if your child's view of you is truly important forever, do you need to be more careful to keep your criticism constructive? If God's perspective is eternally crucial, do your priorities need an overhaul?

CHAPTER 3
The Head

THE POINT: Leading your family like Jesus involves more than emotions and good intentions. It takes thought and planning, too.

GRAND OPENING
Getting Your Thoughts Together

Family Values
by Ken Blanchard

What's the purpose of your family? What's your picture of the future? What's your picture of the future? What values will guide your journey? What goals do you want family members to focus on today?

If you can't answer those questions, you don't have a compelling vision. Without clear vision and direction, the rest of your parenting skills and effort won't matter. You can't be a servant leader if there's nothing to serve.

If you cut children loose without any direction or guidelines, they'll lose their way. The family unit will be fractured as everyone heads off in the direction that he or she decides is best. Guidelines are boundaries

---

that channel energy in a certain direction. It's like a river. If you take away the banks, it won't be a river anymore; it will be a large puddle, devoid of momentum and direction. What keeps the river flowing are its banks, its boundaries.

In companies, people look to the leader for vision and direction. In families, that role falls to the parents. . . .

Once vision and direction are set, children are expected to be responsive—that is, to live according to your guidelines.

Again, you can't be a servant-leader if you don't take care of the leadership part. Don't be afraid of this role. It's not about being bossy; it's about setting up your family to win.[7]

Do you think parents in our culture 100 years ago led more with their hearts or their heads? Do you think that's changed? Why? When it comes to setting family vision and direction, would you prefer a return to the "good old days," or a "new and improved" approach? Why?

WATCH THIS!
Viewing and Discussing the Video

In this portion of the video, Ken outlines the need to discover your family's values and mission and start turning them into a plan. Tricia describes how parents can set priorities as Jesus did—saying yes to the best and no to the rest. Phil talks about how parents can turn these priorities into action in everyday life.

After viewing the authors' presentations, use questions like the following to help you think through what you saw and heard.

1. Ken Blanchard has worked hard to cast a vision for his family members and lead them toward specific goals. How does that compare with the family in which you grew up? How does it compare with the one you're leading now?

2. Read Micah 6:8. Would this make a good statement of your family's values? Why or why not? Is there anything in the Bible that *doesn't* belong in your family's values? Should all Christian families have the same values? Why or why not?

3. How would you prioritize the following, from most important to least? How would you expect a family with those priorities to spend a typical Saturday?
   - feeding starving people in Africa
   - playing games together

- staying physically fit
- keeping your sense of humor
- telling people how to become a Christian

4. In the book *Lead Your Family Like Jesus*, Tricia Goyer points out that parents need to tell their kids specifically what carrying out family priorities looks like. What would you tell your kids that the following look like?
   - clean dishes
   - a mowed lawn
   - brushed teeth
   - respect for brothers and sisters
   - prayer

5. For Jesus' earthly parents, would you say the following were crises or bumps in the road? How might you have reacted to these events?
   - Mary becomes pregnant even though she's a virgin (Luke 1:26-38).

- Mary is about to give birth, but she and Joseph have no place to stay (Luke 2:6-7).
- After Jesus is born, an angel tells Joseph to take Mary and the baby to Egypt (Matthew 2:13-15).
- When Jesus is 12, they lose Him in Jerusalem (Luke 2:41-50).
- While Mary and Jesus are at a wedding, the hosts run out of wine (John 2:1-11).
- Jesus' own brothers don't believe in Him (John 7:5).

6. Phil Hodges urges parents not to let minor problems like childish carelessness distract them from pursuing family goals. Which of the following would you add to the list of things that tend to distract you from keeping your family moving in the right direction?
   - chores
   - TV or Internet
   - school or church activities
   - sports or hobbies
   - earning a living
   - other _____

To Do or Not to Do
by Tricia Goyer

Jesus set priorities for Himself, for His disciples, and for us—many of them nonnegotiable. . . . Here's just one case in point:

> [Jesus'] brothers said, "Why don't you leave here and go up to the Feast so your disciples can get a good look at the works you do? No one who intends to be publicly known does everything behind the scenes. If you're serious about what you are doing, come out in the open and show the world." His brothers were pushing him like this because they didn't believe in him either.
>
> Jesus came back at them, "Don't crowd me. This isn't my time. It's your time—it's *always* your time; you have nothing to lose. The world has nothing against you, but it's up in arms against me. It's against me because I expose the evil behind its pretensions. You go ahead, go up to the Feast. Don't wait for me. I'm not ready. It's not the right time for me." (John 7:1-8, MSG)

Jesus filled His schedule and picked His battles according to His priorities—choosing on one day to heal, on another to teach, on another to spend time alone with His Father. Doing the same in your family will show your kids how to live out your family values, allow them to be accountable, and help you measure their progress.

True success in servant leadership depends on how clearly the values are defined, ordered, and lived by the leader.[8]

If a reality TV show crew had followed your family around last week, what might viewers guess was your top priority as a parent? Why?

SO WHAT?

Connecting Principles to Parenting

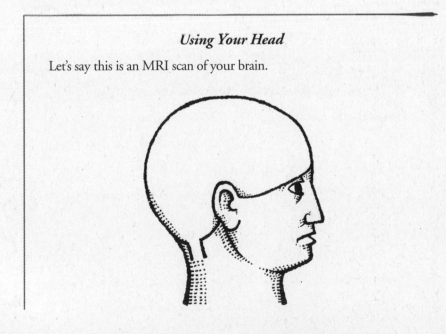

Using Your Head

Let's say this is an MRI scan of your brain.

And let's say this is a list of the Top Ten issues a parent might think about.

Family Vision	Germs
Family Goals	Video Games
Family Values	Report Cards
Family Purpose	Macaroni and Cheese
Family Priorities	Memorizing Bible Verses

Decide what percentage of your brainpower you've been devoting to each issue. Divide the "MRI" into ten compartments to show how you've been "using your head."

What do you think and feel about your answers?

Based on what you've been learning, in what areas might you want to think a little harder? Why?

Staying on Course
by Phil Hodges

Some days being a servant leader [when my kids were young] wasn't easy. Some days I made the wrong choice. One thing that helped me with decision-making was realizing the distinction between deliberate and accidental acts.

Don't you hate it when your kids spill their milk? Me, too. There were times I'd get so frustrated. *Don't they know better?*

As a father I had to learn the difference between accidents and misconduct. There are two ways to look at spilled milk. There's the milk spilled because the cup is too large for a young child to handle, or it gets set down wrong or bumped against a plate. Then there's the milk that spills when your child looks you in the eye, cocks an eyebrow, and turns over a cup. Two different actions, two different heart attitudes.

Sometimes we forget this—especially when it concerns something much bigger than milk. . . .

Every child makes mistakes, and most aren't fatal. When it comes to spilled milk . . . we can either focus on the mess—or we can keep the consistency of purpose in our parenting.[9]

This week, make some coupons on index cards or slips of paper that allow your kids to get away with specific "bumps in the road." Here are a few samples:

This coupon entitles the bearer to receive mercy when accidentally spilling the milk, washing light and dark clothing in the same load of laundry, or filling the kitchen with the smell of burnt microwave popcorn.

This coupon entitles the bearer to "unsay" something that he or she shouldn't have said in the first place.

This coupon entitles the bearer to cancellation of a debt to his or her parents which does not exceed a value of $10.

This coupon entitles the bearer to disappoint his or her parents with a lower-than-expected grade on one homework assignment, an unusual hairstyle or hair color, or failure to eat a vegetable at one meal.

Be sure to explain why you're passing out these "free passes": as a reminder that you want your home to be a place where people can make mistakes and get a second chance, the kind of grace God has offered us through Jesus.

CHAPTER 4

The Hands

THE POINT: Your family will benefit from your attitudes about leadership only when you take action. If you have a servant heart and point of view, you'll become a performance coach.

GRAND OPENING
Getting Your Thoughts Together

For a Limited Time Only
by Tricia Goyer

Jesus knew how brief His "window" of earthly ministry would be, and led His followers accordingly. We don't know that much about our own futures, but a little math makes it clear that our most active parenting years are few. . . .

No one wants to go through a near-death experience, but that's what happened to my friend Ocieanna. This young mom of four was having an ordinary Saturday night when her heart stopped. One minute she was watching television with her husband; the next she gasped, gagged, and slumped over with no pulse. . . .

Prayers went out all over the world. Despite the fact that her heart stopped a second time, less than a week later she came to [from an induced coma]. Ocieanna was confused, but everyone knew she was going to be all right when her friends and family were gathered in her hospital room and she started introducing those who hadn't met each other.

I never would have called Ocieanna a self-serving parent. Yet I can say that her near-death experience brought change. She cut out activities and has more down time with her kids. She's less stressed about her housework and more focused on her family.

Recently Ocieanna and I were writing a novel together. When I mentioned one day that we had a lot to do and not nearly enough time, she sent me a quick note: "I'm not worried about it. I almost died, and I make a point of not worrying about these things."

Her words calmed my heart. Each day—even busy, tiring, emotional days with our kids—is a day we need to be thankful for.[10]

On what day of the year do you tend to value your kids most? Their birthdays? Christmas? New Year's Eve? The first day of school? The anniversary of September 11, 2001? Why?

When time with your kids is precious, how does it tend to shape the way you lead your family? Is that usually a good thing? Why or why not?

WATCH THIS!
Viewing and Discussing the Video

In this portion of the video, Tricia explains why it's vital for parents to make the most of the fleeting childrearing years—and how Jesus provided a blueprint in His use of time. Ken notes the importance of helping kids succeed through coaching; Phil shows how emulating Jesus inspires obedience instead of rebellion in kids.

After viewing the authors' presentations, use questions like the following to help you think through what you saw and heard.

1. How much time do you have left to influence your kids before they're on their own? Only God knows that, of course. But take the number of years expected to pass before your children leave home; multiply it by 52 to get the number of weeks; multiply that by 168 to see the number of hours. Now divide that by the estimated number of hours you spend with each child in an average week. How do you feel about the result? Is it more, less, or about the same as Jesus probably spent with His disciples during His three-year earthly ministry? Do you find that encouraging, scary, depressing, or challenging?

2. Read Ephesians 5:15. How does this apply to parenting? What opportunities to influence your child are you likely to encounter this week at each of the following times? How can you "make the most" of them?
   - dinner time
   - bedtime
   - wake-up time

3. How do you decide what your child needs to learn in order to be prepared for life? How do you know which principles need to be taught first?

4. Ken encourages parents to be "performance coaches." That involves goal setting, praising progress, and reprimanding or redirecting when progress isn't being made. What kind of goal, praise, and redirection would you use in each of the following situations?
   - You want to teach your four-year-old to pick up his toys.
   - You want your 17-year-old to decide whether to attend community college before the application deadline arrives in a month.

- You want your 10-year-old to empathize with other people's feelings—starting with dropping the habit of calling his little sister "Jabba the Gut."

5. How did Jesus inspire His disciples to obey Him? Based on what you know about Him—whether it's a little or a lot—which of the following would you expect Him to do, and which would you expect Him to avoid? Why?
   - giving His followers a pomegranate when they cooperated with each other
   - using the "silent treatment" when they broke a commandment
   - letting them suffer the natural consequences of trying to lord it over each other
   - demonstrating obedience to His Father by asking to be baptized
   - persuading them with interesting stories
   - calling them "losers" when they disappointed Him

6. In the book *Lead Your Family Like Jesus*, Phil Hodges gives parents six tips for inspiring obedience:

   1. Stand your ground when your child challenges you.
   2. Don't let fear set your agenda.
   3. Tailor your tactics to fit the child.
   4. Model obedience yourself.
   5. Build trust with love, explanations, and apologies.
   6. Test to make sure the child understands your expectations.

   Did you use one of these last week? If so, what happened? Which would you most like to try this week?

Teaching to the Test
by Ken Blanchard

When I was a college professor, I was periodically in trouble with the faculty. That's because at the beginning of the class, I often handed my students the final exam. When the other teachers found out about that, they asked, "What are you *doing*?"

"I'm confused," I'd tell them. "I thought we were supposed to teach our students."

"We are. But don't give them the final exam ahead of time!"

I'd smile. "Not only will I give them the final exam on the first day of class, but what do you think I'm going to do all semester? I'm going to teach them the answers, so when they get to the final exam, they'll get As."

Life is all about getting As—not maintaining a normal distribution curve. I wanted all my students to win. That's exactly what Jesus wants—all of us to win. He never believed in a normal distribution curve. He wanted everyone to win and become His disciples. . . .

When it comes to coaching, it's important to follow Jesus' model. He was clear about the leadership aspect of servant leadership—why He came, what the good news was, and what He wanted people to do. He modeled the servant aspect of servant leadership with everyone He met.

He told His followers, "Go and make disciples of all nations."

Why? Because He wanted everybody to win.[11]

Given the limited time in which parents can influence their children, how could this approach help? Would it work better with some aspects of parenting than others? Why?

Everybody Wins

Goal: To teach your child to spend money wisely.

Strategy: Reveal the answers in advance so that your child "passes the test."

What answers would you reveal in the following areas? In other words, what principles (each of which should be no longer than ten words) would you share with your child?

1. Planning and patience vs. instant gratification

2. Saving up vs. borrowing money

3. Shopping wisely vs. impulse buying

4. Analyzing advertising vs. believing the hype

5. Learning contentment vs. always wanting more

How would you make sure your child understood these answers?

What opportunities would you give your child to see them
in action?

How would you help him or her to practice the principles?

What kind of "test" could you provide to show that your child had
learned the answers?

Follow Me
by Phil Hodges

Obedience is first and foremost a matter of the heart. It can be described as an internal desire to willingly respond in trust and respect when called to action. It involves wanting to do what's required. Obedience is not a natural response of our hearts or the hearts of our children. It cannot be forced or coerced; it must be nurtured as a choice.

Obedience goes beyond compliance and conformity. There's a strong temptation to measure the success of our parenting by the external behavior of our children: If they do what they're told, say their prayers, stop rolling their eyes every time we ask them to do something, exhibit good manners outside the home, and eventually get a scholarship to their college of choice, we may be inclined to take credit for a parenting job well done. If the primary means we use to that end are rewards and consequences, though, we can send our kids off with a "What's in it for me?" approach toward life choices.

When my daughter LeeAnne was three years old, she expressed the essence of the parental obedience challenge when she told my wife, Jane, "Mommy, I can't wanna do it!"

We're called to help our children "wanna do it" for the right reasons.[12]

This week you'll be "in the trenches" as a parent. It may be easy to forget Tricia Goyer's insight: "Each day—even busy, tiring, emotional days with our kids—is a day we need to be thankful for." How could you remind yourself that every minute you spend with your child is precious?

Come up with a memory-jogger that does just that. This might be your child's photo taped to your car's steering wheel, or—if you're married—a code word your spouse says to you when family stress is getting you down. Or it could be an alarm set on a cell phone or watch, or something you'll wear—maybe a rubber wristband or a tie your child gave you. Whatever you choose, let it remind you that you have "a limited time only" to take action on what you've learned.

CHAPTER 5
The Habits

THE POINT: Habits like spending time in solitude, prayer, and practicing forgiveness and grace help you stay committed to leading your family like Jesus.

GRAND OPENING
Getting Your Thoughts Together

> ### Time with God: a Dad's Perspective
> #### by Ken Blanchard
>
> In our Lead Like Jesus Encounter workshops, we ask participants to take forty-five minutes of solitude—a time when they don't talk to anyone, use their computers or cell phones, or have any other distractions.
>
> We ask them to begin by putting their hands, palms down, on their knees and thinking of anything they're concerned about. As a concern appears in their mind, they mentally put it down at the foot of the Cross. When they have completed thinking about their concerns, they turn their hands upward in a posture of receiving, contemplating some aspect of the character of God—such as His

---

mercy, love, grace, or power. We encourage them to listen without any agenda.

Before we send people off for their period of solitude, we have them recite Psalm 46:10 with us in this way: *Be still and know that I am God. Be still and know. Be still. Be.*

When people return from their solitude, they have big smiles on their faces. While many of them find it difficult to quiet their minds, they say it was a powerful experience.

The reality is that most of us spend little, if any, time in solitude. Yet if we don't, how can God have a chance to talk with us?[13]

Does solitude feel to you more like a reward or a punishment? Why? What do you think would be the ideal amount to have in a day? How does that compare with the amount you usually have? If you had more, what would you do with it?

WATCH THIS!
Viewing and Discussing the Video

In this portion of the video, Ken provides a dad's view of how to stay on track by staying close to God—as Jesus did—through spiritual disciplines like Bible study and prayer. Tricia shares a mom's perspective on meeting challenges by meeting with our heavenly Father—following Jesus' example of pursuing solitude and prayer. Phil explains how parents can turn family members' mistakes into growth opportunities through Jesus-like forgiveness and grace.

After viewing the authors' presentations, use questions like the following to help you think through what you saw and heard.

1. What do you think was Ken's best suggestion on how parents can spend time with God? What would you add to it from your own experience?

2. If Jesus gave a press conference during His earthly ministry, how do you think He might answer the following questions from reporters?
   - "How come You don't heal everybody? Doesn't everyone deserve Your help?"
   - "Why do You keep going off by Yourself? Aren't You a people person?"
   - "You seem to spend an awful lot of time praying. Shouldn't You be doing something more constructive?"
   - "You've surrounded Yourself with a little group of yes-men. Why don't You get input from others who might disagree with You?"

3. Which of the following do you tend to assume about those who talk about "spiritual disciplines," have daily devotions, try to read through the Bible in a year, keep records of answered prayer, or watch sermons on the Internet?
    • They have a lot of time on their hands.
    • They must not have young children.
    • They're boring.
    • They're really old.
    • They're way out of my league.
    • other _____

    Does Tricia seem to fit these stereotypes? Why or why not?

4. Tricia has written that Phil Hodges prayed for the future spouses of his children from the time they were little. If you did that, how often would you do it? What would you pray about those future spouses?

5. Phil has said that "Grace plus anything else equals anything but grace." What do you think he means? In each of the following situations, what is the "anything else"?

- A mom is willing to forgive her son for accidentally breaking her eyeglasses, but only if he apologizes first.
- A dad praises one son for his soccer exploits, but ignores the other son's singing ability.
- A mom hugs her teenage daughter when the girl lets Mom pick out school clothes, but not when the daughter insists on choosing her own.
- A dad offers to take his overweight son to a concert if the boy will "just lose a few pounds."

6. If grace is "unmerited favor," what undeserved but positive response could you make to a child who does the following—without encouraging a repeat of the child's behavior?
   - says, "I hate you!"
   - forgets your birthday—two years in a row
   - uses a racial slur to refer to a neighbor
   - gets pregnant—or causes a pregnancy

Moving On
by Phil Hodges

Unlike Jesus, we all fall short of 100 percent in our journey as leaders. This is especially true in our role as parents. Sometimes we make mistakes that could have been avoided. Sometimes we say or do things in the heat of the moment that we regret. If our egos are wrapped up in our performance and the opinions of others, we'll be unable to forgive our own shortcomings—let alone anyone else's.

An unforgiving heart is not capable of leading like Jesus at home or anywhere else. It will always look backward to justify not moving forward in a relationship. An unforgiving heart stores up resentment and marinates in bitterness. It's stingy with praise and microscopic in its judgment and suspicion of others. It will isolate its owner and cause him or her to wear the attitude of a martyr or victim in dealing with others.

Leaders seeking to grow and develop people need a healthy capacity to forgive, correct, and move on. As family leaders, we can be sure that everyone we deal with, including ourselves, is going to make mistakes or otherwise disappoint us. . . .

Forgiveness is a hallmark of what it means to lead like Jesus. He taught it to His disciples, and He practiced it toward those who betrayed Him. He grants forgiveness willingly to those who accept the gift of His sacrifice.

By practicing grace and forgiveness, we can create harmony in our homes. When we forgive with grace, we model the essence of what Jesus was all about.[14]

Have you ever thought of grace and forgiveness as habits? Why or why not?

How has someone else's willingness to forgive you and "move on" benefited you? What might be the next opportunity you'll have to do that for your child?

SO WHAT?
Connecting Principles to Parenting

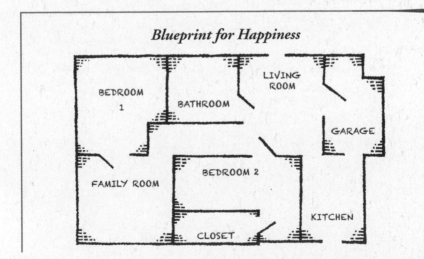

Blueprint for Happiness

BEDROOM 1

BATHROOM

LIVING ROOM

GARAGE

FAMILY ROOM

BEDROOM 2

KITCHEN

CLOSET

Pretend this is a map of your home. Draw stick figures to show the best places for you to practice solitude, to pray, to read the Bible, and to show more grace and forgiveness where it tends to be needed.

If you tried to do these things this week, how do you think it would turn out? Why?

What obstacles stand in the way?

Who could help you remove them?

How could your family make it easier to try these things?

How could you ask for your family members' help?

Time with God: a Mom's Perspective
by Tricia Goyer

Nobody seems to know who said this, but it's worth listening to: "One should never initiate anything that he cannot saturate with prayer." This couldn't be more true when it comes to parenting and becoming servant-leaders in our homes.

If solitude is the most elusive of the habits for us to develop, prayer is the one that requires the most unlearning of old habits. Our prayer practices tend to be based on the traditions we grew up with, whether or not they help us and our families grow closer to God. . . .

[When] I became a mom . . . I learned that prayer is a conversation that can take place all day long. Yes, we can pray during those quiet morning hours—but we also can pray in the carpool lane or as we pile items into our grocery cart.

Prayer is an essential act of the will that demonstrates whether we're really serious about living and leading our families like Jesus. Without it we'll never be able to connect our plans and efforts with God's plan for His kingdom, or engage the spiritual resources Jesus promised in the work of the Holy Spirit. Seeking God's will through prayer, waiting in faith for an answer, acting in accordance with that answer, and being at peace with the outcome, call for a level of spiritual maturity that will keep any parent seeking to lead like Jesus in the posture of a lifelong learner.[15]

Want to pick up a *good* habit? Choose either prayer or Bible reading—and three times you'll do one or the other this week for five minutes at a time in a particular place.

Bad habits may seem to form themselves. But good habits? Not so much. Commitment to a specific time and place, and repeating the action, is the way to form the kind of habit worth having.

CHAPTER 6
Ready to Lead

THE POINT: Parenting like Jesus is a daily challenge filled with failures and victories. Stick with it, though, and you'll be surprised what God will do through you as you apply these principles to your parenting.

GRAND OPENING
Getting Your Thoughts Together

Got It? A Quick Review
by Phil Hodges

Jesus was a model for "being in the moment." I don't think training His disciples was a hit-and-miss thing. . . . As He walked together with His disciples on the journey of life, Jesus observed them in the moment, listened to them, and answered their questions. . . .

One of my favorite images of a parent in the moment with a child is my sister-in-law, Susanne, talking with her children when they were young. Because of a hearing loss, it's a challenge for her to understand what people are saying unless they're faced directly toward her.

So whenever her little ones wanted to speak with her, Susanne

---

would kneel down, lovingly hold their face with both hands, and listen with her eyes and ears to what they had to say. It's a beautiful picture of listening that we can incorporate into our parenting.

I also like to think of Jesus doing the same thing as we turn to Him for help. Can you picture the tenderness in His eyes? Can you imagine His desire to lead you with tender care?

Leading your family like Jesus starts with being led by Jesus. Being led by Jesus is all about turning to Him, following Him, and knowing He's not only walking beside you on your journey as a parent; He's doing so with tender, loving care.[16]

If you could see Jesus "walking beside you on your journey as a parent," what do you think His expression and tone of voice might be? How might being able to see Him affect your ability to lead your family?

WATCH THIS!
Viewing and Discussing the Video

In this portion of the video, Phil summarizes how leading like Jesus has helped his family and reviews the main principles of the book. Tricia suggests specific examples of how parents can lead their families like Jesus—such as activities that help her family identify its values and priorities. Ken wraps up the series by motivating parents to exercise the kind of Jesus-like family leadership they've been learning about—reassuring them that, despite obstacles, they can make a big difference in their children's lives by following through and sticking with it.

After viewing the authors' presentations, use questions like the following to help you think through what you saw and heard.

1. Why is it important to keep the Heart, Head, Hands, and Habits aligned in order to lead your family like Jesus? How might a parent's ability to influence his or her kids be affected by each of the following misalignments?
   - Heart but No Head
   - Head but No Heart
   - Heart but No Hands
   - Hands but No Habits

2. Let's say Ken Blanchard, Phil Hodges, and Tricia Goyer are coming to your place for dinner. You want to be able to tell them you learned something from their video series. What will you say? And what will you tell your kids before the three authors come over?

3. The main principles in this course involved eternal perspective, humility, focusing on God and not others, your family mission, priorities, staying on course, making the most of the childrearing years, helping kids succeed, inspiring obedience, staying close to God, and offering forgiveness and grace. If you had to pick just one of these to work on for the next three months, which would it be? What's the first thing you'd do, and what would be your goal for Day Number 90?

4. Which of the following Bible verses would make a good motto for you as a family leader in the months and years ahead? Why?
   • Philippians 1:6
   • Galatians 6:9
   • Hebrews 12:12
   • Ecclesiastes 12:8
   • other _____

5. Twenty years from now, how will you be able to tell whether you succeeded as a family leader?
   • My kids will all be Christians.
   • My kids will be servant leaders themselves.
   • My kids will still be speaking to me.

- My kids won't be on the FBI's Most Wanted list.
- other _____

6. If someday you were inducted into the Family Leaders' Hall of Fame, what three people (other than the authors of *Lead Your Family Like Jesus*) would you give credit to during your acceptance speech? Why? What would you say about the role of Jesus Himself?

Workable Ways to Lead Your Family Like Jesus
by Tricia Goyer

One of the best ways I know to determine your family's values and priorities is through a fun after-dinner activity. Take some food items from your refrigerator or pantry and read the labels together. Some of the words that describe your favorite foods might be "bold," "organic," "flavorful," "healthy," or "classic." Explain how the words on the label represent what's inside.

Next, use poster board and markers to make a sign—a "label"— for your family. How is your family different from others you know? Let younger kids draw pictures of your family to go with the labels. Then ask, "Do the activities we choose fit and reflect our family's label?"

If they don't, discuss what you need to step back from in order to step into what God has designed your family to do.

Once you figure out what needs to be cut out of your lives, consider what activities *would* match what your heart tells you is most important. Write a list of action steps that would lead you to doing what you believe. As you make plans, your family will get a glimpse of who God designed you—as a unit—to be.[17]

What's one simple, practical thing you've done to help your kids develop a character trait, learn a skill, or build closeness? Would you recommend it to other parents? Why or why not?

SO WHAT?
Connecting Principles to Parenting

Yes, We Cans

Come up with "family labels" for these cans by using words from the following list that apply to your family. Use at least three words on each can. Try to concentrate on qualities that may come in handy as you try to carry out principles you've learned from *Lead Your Family Like Jesus*. If you don't find the words you need on the list, use your own.

HUMBLE	ENERGETIC	FEARLESS
HARDWORKING	PERSEVERING	SERVING
HARMONIOUS	CONFIDENT	HOSPITABLE
BRAINY	QUIET	TOUGH
HUMOROUS	LOUD	FLEXIBLE
BOLD	LOYAL	HONEST
CREATIVE	GENEROUS	CAREFUL
PATIENT	GENTLE	OPTIMISTIC
LOVING	JOYFUL	FAITHFUL
MUSICAL	OUTDOORSY	DRAMATIC

What are two other ingredients you might need to follow through on the "recipes" offered in this series?

How might another family help you to develop those two ingredients? For example, if your family is long on enthusiasm but short on organization, could some detail-oriented friends show you how to make a list of steps to reach your goals? Who might those friends be, and how could you get up the courage to ask them?

You Can Do It!
by Ken Blanchard

As you apply the concepts you've learned in this book, remember that parenting like Jesus is a daily journey and challenge rather than a final destination. This journey will always be filled with failures, roughly-right behaviors, and out-and-out victories. To keep on keeping on, we suggest two strategies:

First, pray constantly. Ask God to guide you to the truth that will have the greatest impact on improving the way you parent.

Second, periodically review your progress in parenting like Jesus. Celebrate it, and redirect your efforts when you think you've lapsed.

You'll be surprised what God will do through you as you apply these biblical principles to your parenting. If you want a true picture of how well you're making positive changes, watch the reactions your younger kids have to you. As they get older, ask them for feedback: What's working—and what's not?

To serve your children as Christ serves us means honoring God and His commandments and putting the love of Jesus into your parenting. When you do that, you'll leave a positive legacy for your children, their children, and their children's children.

Trust Jesus as your parenting leadership role model. When you do, you'll make Him smile—and help your children fulfill their heaven-sent potential.[18]

The authors of *Lead Your Family Like Jesus* recommend repeating "affirmations" to yourself when you get up in the morning. These statements can motivate you to tackle the task of family leadership with confidence, relying on God for strength and wisdom. If you'd like to give it a try, pick one of the following and say it each morning this week. Or create your own!

Do not be anxious about anything,
but in everything, by prayer and petition,
with thanksgiving, present your requests to God.
And the peace of God, which transcends all understanding,
will guard your hearts and your minds in Christ Jesus.
(Philippians 4:6-7)

Be still and know that I am God.
Be still and know.
Be still.
Be.
(Based on Psalm 46:10)

Good morning, Daddy! What are You up to today?
How can I help? I'm available.

Lord, clear me out of me. Fill me up with You
and then clothe me with humility.

In the morning I rest my arms awhile on
the windowsill of heaven and gaze upon the face
of the Lord. Then, with that vision in mind,
I turn strong and meet the day.

NOTES

1. Ken Blanchard in *Lead Your Family Like Jesus* by Ken Blanchard, Phil Hodges, and Tricia Goyer (Focus on the Family/ Tyndale House Publishers, 2013), 2-4.
2. Phil Hodges in *Lead Your Family Like Jesus*, 21-23.
3. Tricia Goyer in *Lead Your Family Like Jesus*, 38-39.
4. Blanchard, 10-16.
5. Hodges, 28.
6. Goyer, 34-35.
7. Blanchard, 56-57.
8. Goyer, 61-62.
9. Hodges, 75-79.
10. Goyer, 94-95.
11. Blanchard, 105, 118.
12. Hodges, 123-124.
13. Blanchard, 143.
14. Hodges, 172-173.
15. Goyer, 163-164.
16. Hodges, 185-186.
17. Goyer, 66.
18. Blanchard, 189.

ABOUT OUR PRESENTERS

KEN BLANCHARD, coauthor of *The One Minute Manager®*, *Lead Like Jesus: Lessons for Everyone from the Greatest Leadership Role Model of All Time,* and more than fifty other management and leadership books, is widely characterized as one of the most insightful, powerful, and compassionate people in business today. He is known for his knack for making the seemingly complex easy to understand. Ken is Chief Spiritual Officer of The Ken Blanchard Companies™, a global leader in workplace learning, employee productivity, leadership, and team effectiveness. He cofounded the company with Margie Blanchard, his wife of fifty years. Their children, Scott and Debbie, have played major roles in making The Ken Blanchard Companies the most admired firm in its industry. Ken, along with Phil Hodges, is also the cofounder of Lead Like Jesus, a nonprofit ministry.

PHIL HODGES, a lifelong friend of Ken Blanchard, served as a human resource and industrial relations manager in corporate America for 36 years with Xerox Corporation and U.S. Steel. During his career at Xerox, Phil served as chief negotiator for fifty collective bargaining agreements and as the senior human resources manager for a thousand-employee manufacturing operation.

As chairman of his local church elder council for six years, Phil developed a passion for bringing effective leadership principles into the life of the local church. He and his family served on short-term mission projects both in the USA and internationally. In 1999, Phil and Ken cofounded Lead Like Jesus where Phil has served as its first managing director and as chief content officer. He and Ken Blanchard have coauthored five books: *Lead Like Jesus: Lessons from the Greatest Leadership Role Model of All Time; The Most Loving Place in Town: A Modern Day Parable for the Church; Leadership Development for Every Day of the Year; The Servant Leader;* and *Leadership by the Book* (with Bill Hybels). Phil and his wife, Jane Kinnaird Hodges, live in southern California, where they enjoy daily interaction and involvement in the lives of their two married children, their children's spouses, and seven grandchildren.

TRICIA GOYER is a bestselling author of more than thirty novels, including *Night Song*, which was awarded American Christian Fiction Writers' 2005 Book of the Year for Long Historical Romance, and *Dawn of a Thousand Nights*, which won the same award in 2006. Her coauthored novel *The Swiss Courier* was a Christy Award nominee. She has also authored nine nonfiction books and more than three hundred articles for national publications. In 2003, Tricia was one of two authors named "Writer of the Year" at the Mount Hermon Christian Writer's Conference, and she has been interviewed by *Focus on the Family*, *Moody Mid-Day Connection*, *The Harvest Show*, *NBC's Monday Today*, *Aspiring Women*, and hundreds of other radio and television stations. Tricia and her husband, John, have four children and one grandchild and live in Arkansas.

LEAD YOUR FAMILY LIKE JESUS BOOK AND GROUP VIDEO CURRICULUM $10 REBATE

GET A $10 REBATE

when you purchase both the *Lead Your Family Like Jesus Group Experience* and *Lead Your Family Like Jesus* hardcover book. Both titles must be purchased at a retail store to qualify. Simply return the completed rebate form (original or photocopy), the original dated

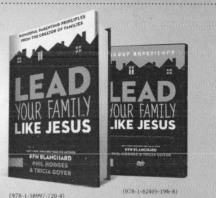

(978-1-58997-720-4)

(978-1-62405-196-8)

store receipt(s) for both products, and the UPC bar code from both packages (original or photocopy) to: Lead Your Family Like Jesus Rebate, Attn. Customer Service, 351 Executive Dr., Carol Stream, IL 60188.

NAME _____

ADDRESS _____

CITY _____ STATE _____ ZIP _____

E-MAIL ADDRESS _____

STORE WHERE PURCHASED _____

SIGNATURE _____

The Family project™
A Divine Reflection

INTRODUCING THE GROUNDBREAKING FOLLOW-UP
TO FOCUS ON THE FAMILY'S THE TRUTH PROJECT®

THE PROFOUND IMPACT OF BIBLICAL FAMILIES

From the creators of the life-changing series *Focus on the Family's The Truth Project®* comes a stunning new journey of discovery that explores family as a revelation of God—and the extraordinary impact families have on the world around them. Introducing *The Family Project™*, a transformative, feature-length documentary and DVD curriculum that reveals—through an in-depth exploration of God's design and purpose—biblical truths about the role of families in society.

VISIT
FamilyProject.com
TO LEARN MORE

FOCUS ON THE FAMILY®

Welcome to the Family

Whether you purchased this book, borrowed it, or received it as a gift, thanks for reading it! This is just one of many insightful, biblically based resources that Focus on the Family produces for people in all stages of life.

Focus is a global Christian ministry dedicated to helping families thrive as they celebrate and cultivate God's design for marriage and experience the adventure of parenthood. Our outreach exists to support individuals and families in the joys and challenges they face, and to equip and empower them to be the best they can be.

Through our many media outlets, we offer help and hope, promote moral values and share the life-changing message of Jesus Christ with people around the world.

Focus on the Family MAGAZINES

These faith-building, character-developing publications address the interests, issues, concerns, and challenges faced by every member of your family from preschool through the senior years.

For More INFORMATION

ONLINE:
Log on to
FocusOnTheFamily.com
In Canada, log on to
FocusOnTheFamily.ca

PHONE:
Call toll-free:
**800-A-FAMILY
(232-6459)**
In Canada, call toll-free:
800-661-9800

THRIVING FAMILY®	**FOCUS ON THE FAMILY CLUBHOUSE JR.®**	**FOCUS ON THE FAMILY CLUBHOUSE®**	**FOCUS ON THE FAMILY CITIZEN®**
Marriage & Parenting	Ages 4 to 8	Ages 8 to 12	U.S. news issues

Rev. 3/11

LOOKING FOR YOUR
NEXT STEPS?

CEO or teacher, pastor or parent, shopkeeper or student—
if you desire to impact the lives of others by leading like Jesus,
we invite you to join the LLJ movement and expand your leadership
abilities. Lead Like Jesus offers leadership-building resources for
teens and young adults as well as for seasoned executives, all
with the goal of demonstrating God's love for people while
helping them change the way they live, love, and lead.

The following products are available for purchase at
www.LeadLikeJesus.com

SIGN UP TO RECEIVE THE
E-DEVOTION

*Sign up to receive a brief, insightful,
challenging reflection three times a
week in your inbox—a great way to
learn more about leading like Jesus.*

CONTINUE YOUR PERSONAL
GROWTH BY PURCHASING
LLJ STUDY GUIDES

*Containing personal reflections,
memory verses, prayers, activities
and guidelines for creating your
own leadership plan. These study
guides contain lessons for anyone
who aspires to lead like Jesus.*

ENGAGE THE NEXT GENERATION THROUGH
STUDENT RESOURCES

*Learning to lead like Jesus is an
ongoing pursuit. LLJ materials for
students are designed to foster
life-changing leadership habits
and develop skills early that will
last a lifetime.*

PARTICIPATE IN A
HIGH-IMPACT WORKSHOP—
ATTEND AN
ENCOUNTER

*An interactive program,
Encounter helps leaders
create positive change in
both their personal and
professional relationships.*

INCREASE YOUR PERSONAL
GROWTH THROUGH
ACCELERATE™

*Accelerate combines written
content, video, and powerful
questions to foster continued
growth as a LLJ leader. An
online program delivered daily
and built to move at a speed
that's right for you.*

LEAD LIKE JESUS